CORAL REEF

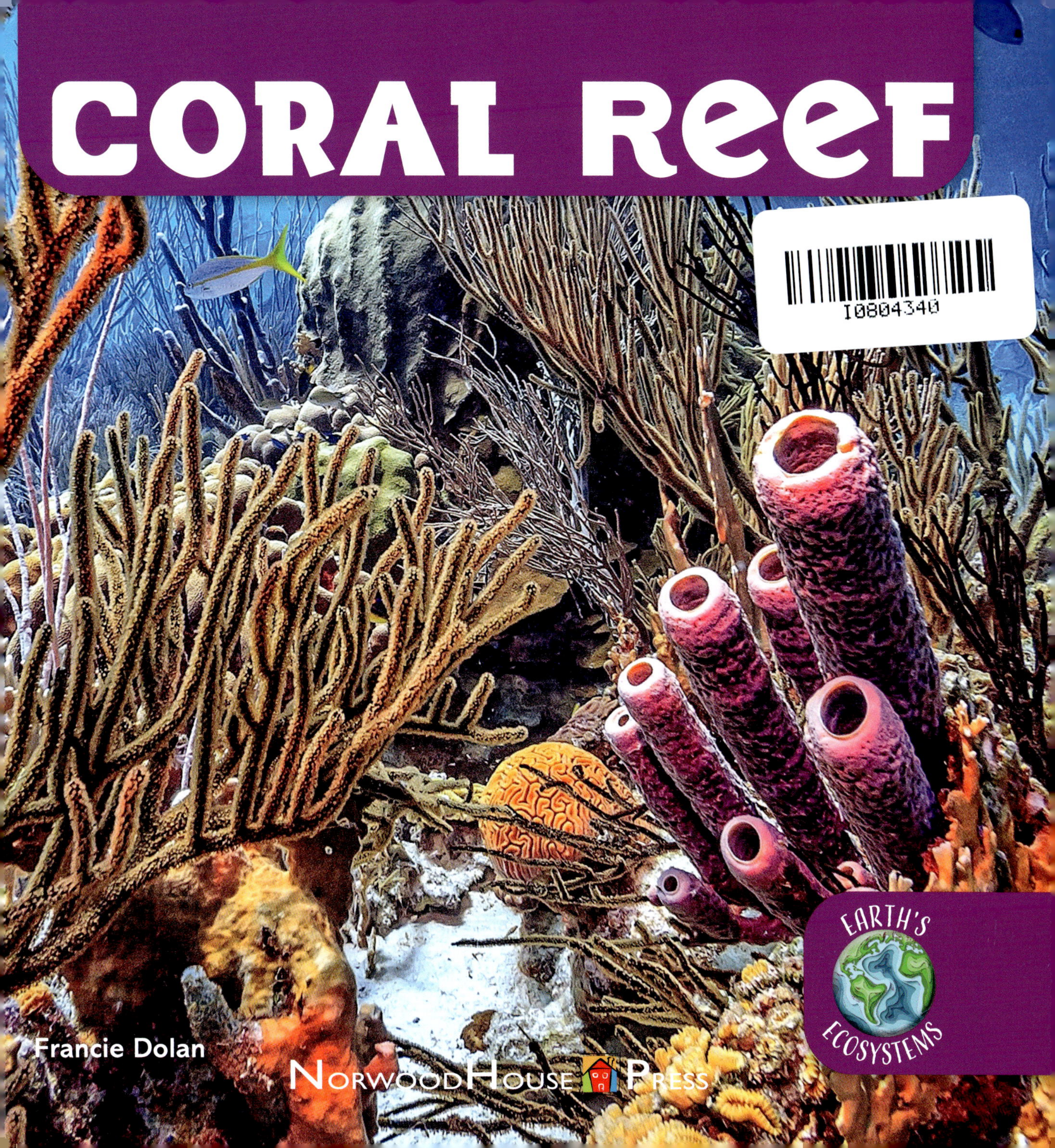

Francie Dolan

NORWOOD HOUSE PRESS

EARTH'S ECOSYSTEMS

Cataloging-in-Publication Data

Names: Dolan, Francie.
Title: Coral reef / Francie Dolan.
Description: Buffalo, NY : Norwood House Press, 2026. | Series: Earth's ecosystems | Includes glossary and index.
Identifiers: ISBN 9781978577107 (pbk.) | ISBN 9781978577114 (library bound) | ISBN 9781978577121 (ebook)
Subjects: LCSH: Coral reef ecology--Juvenile literature. | Coral reefs and islands--Juvenile literature.
Classification: LCC QH541.5.C7 D65 2026 | DDC 577.789--dc23

Published in 2026 by
Norwood House Press
2544 Clinton Street
Buffalo, NY 14224

Designer: Rhea Magaro
Editor: Kim Thompson

Photo credits: Cover, p1. John A. Anderson, Kumer Oksa-na/Shutterstock.com; pp. 3, 16 John A. Ander-son/Shutterstock.com; p. 4 Qasimphotographer/Shutterstock.com; p. 5 Kichigin/Shutterstock.com; p. 6 Mathias Berlin, DES-SIGNSTUNN/Shutterstock.com; p. 7 Andrei Armiagov/Shutterstock.com; p. 9 Ingrid Rousseau/Shutterstock.com; p. 10 Citrus deliciosa/Shutterstock.com; p. 11 Ethan Daniels/Shutterstock.com; p. 12 Lukas Gojda/Shutterstock.com; p. 13 Angela N Perryman/Shutterstock.com; p. 15 DiveSpin.Com/Shutterstock.com; p. 17 Kurit afshen/Shutterstock.com; p. 18 QuolaLens/Shutterstock.com; p. 19 Chai Seamaker/Shutterstock.com; p. 19 Damsea/Shutterstock.com; p. 21 Richard Whit-combe/Shutterstock.com

Printed in the United States of America

CPSIA compliance information: Batch #CWNHP26: For further information contact Norwood House Press at 1-800-237-9932.

TABLE OF CONTENTS

The Coral Reef Ecosystem

Eco- means "home" or "environment." *System* means "a group of things that work together." Earth has many **ecosystems** that support life. Each is home to a network of living things that depend on each other.

One kind of ecosystem is a coral reef. Coral reefs are rock-like formations in warm, shallow, ocean waters. They are made from the skeletons of tiny creatures called coral **polyps**.

Over thousands of years, coral reefs can grow into vast structures. The Great Barrier Reef near Australia is the largest coral reef in the world.

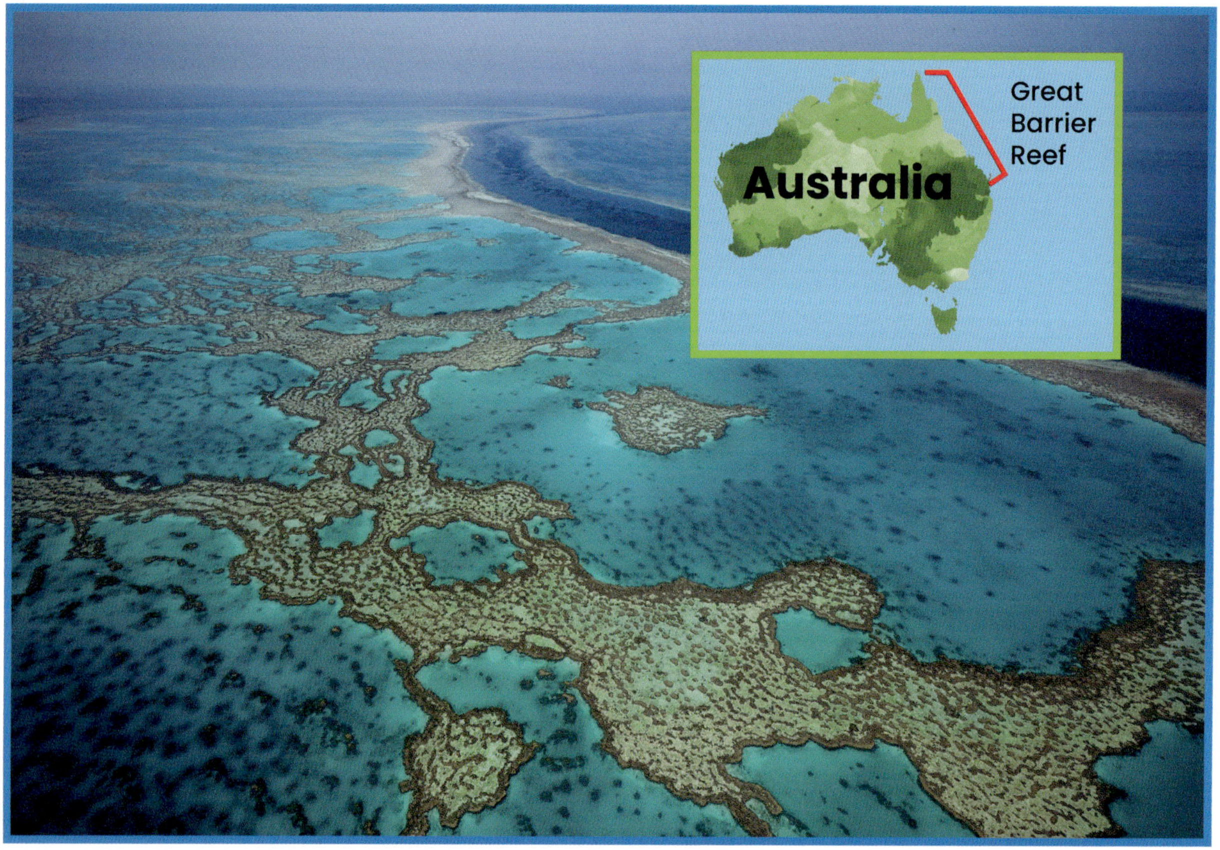

Coral reefs have amazing **biodiversity**. Although they cover just one percent of the seafloor, 25 percent of all ocean **species** depend on them for food and shelter.

Coral Reef Plants

Special **adaptations** help **marine** plants grow in and around coral reefs.

Zooxanthellae are microscopic **algae** that form a **symbiosis** with coral polyps. The coral protects the algae and produces carbon dioxide. The algae use the carbon dioxide to make food and oxygen for the coral.

Seagrasses have strong roots that anchor them to the ocean floor. Their thin, flexible leaves sway in ocean currents.

Vast seagrass meadows grow near coral reefs. Many animals hide in them and use them to protect their babies.

Coral Reef Animals

Many animals have adapted to living near coral reefs.

Manta rays are experts at finding food on reefs. Their sieve-like mouths filter the water for tiny living things.

Coral reefs have many bright colors. The stonefish fits right in. Its **camouflage** lets it hide from predators and sneak up on prey.

Sea anemones attach themselves to coral reefs. Their stinging **tentacles** catch prey.

The clownfish has a layer of skin that protects it from the anemone's sting. The fish hides among the anemone's tentacles. It attacks animals that try to eat the anemone.

Coral Reef Food Chains

On a coral reef, living things eat other living things in food chains. A clam might eat algae. A jellyfish may eat the clam.

A sea turtle might make a meal of the jellyfish. After the turtle dies, a sea cucumber on the ocean floor may eat its remains.

All living things in coral reef ecosystems depend on each other for survival. These places are important for plants, animals, and planet Earth.

Glossary

adaptations (ad-ap-TAY-shuhns): physical or behavioral changes that help plants and animals survive in their environment

algae (AL-jee): small plants without roots or stems

biodiversity (bye-oh-duh-VUR-si-tee): a wide variety of species living in a single area

camouflage (KAM-uh-flahzh): a disguise or natural coloring that lets animals hide by making them look like their surroundings

ecosystems (EE-koh-sis-tuhms): natural communities where plants, animals, and their environment all work together

marine (muh-REEN): of or having to do with the ocean

polyps (PAH-luhps): small sea animals with tubular bodies and round mouths surrounded by tentacles

species (SPEE-sheez): a group of living things that are alike and can reproduce together

symbiosis (sim-bee-OH-suhs): two living things that stay close because each benefits the other

tentacles (TEN-tuh-kuhlz): long, flexible limbs that may be used to feel, grasp, and sting prey

Thinking Questions

1. What is an ecosystem?
2. Why are coral reefs important?
3. Give an example of an adaptation that helps coral reef plants survive.
4. Give an example of an adaptation that helps coral reef animals survive.
5. What does a food chain show?

Index

About the Author

Francie Dolan is continually amazed by the natural world and how Earth's plants, animals, and natural resources are interconnected. From her home near Seattle, Washington, she loves to hike and explore forests, lakes, mountains, and the seashore. When she gets home, she likes to draw and write about what she sees on her adventures.